D0327913

Real People

Benjamin Franklin

By Philip Abraham

Children's Press®
A Division of Scholastic Inc.
New York / Toronto / London / Auckland / Sydney
Mexico City / New Delhi / Hong Kong
Danbury, Connecticut

Photo Credits: Cover © The Corcoran Gallery of Art/Corbis; p. 5 © Francis G. Mayer/Corbis; p. 7 © Corbis; pp. 9, 11, 15, 17, 19, 21 © Bettmann/Corbis; p. 13 © Hulton/Archive by Getty Images

Contributing Editor: Jennifer Silate
Book Design: Christopher Logan

Library of Congress Cataloging-in-Publication Data

Abraham, Philip, 1970–
Benjamin Franklin / by Philip Abraham.
p. cm. -- (Real people)
Includes index.
Summary: An easy-to-read biography of the man who was a publisher, inventor, scientist, and one of the authors of the Declaration of Independence.
ISBN 0-516-23954-6 (lib. bdg.) -- ISBN 0-516-23601-6 (pbk.)
1. Franklin, Benjamin, 1706–1790--Juvenile literature. 2. Statesmen--United States--Biography--Juvenile literature. 3. Scientists--United States--Biography--Juvenile literature. 4. Inventors--United States--Biography--Juvenile literature. 5. Printers--United States--Biography--Juvenile literature. [1. Franklin, Benjamin, 1706–1790. 2. Statesmen. 3. Scientists. 4. Inventors. 5. Printers.] I. Title. II. Real people (Children's Press)

E302.6.F8 A185 2002
973.3'092--dc21
[B]

2001047086

Copyright © 2002 by Rosen Book Works, Inc.
All rights reserved. Published simultaneously in Canada.
Printed in Perú.
8 9 10 R 11 10 09 08 07 06

Contents

1	Meet Benjamin Franklin	4
2	Printing	8
3	Inventing	16
4	New Words	22
5	To Find Out More	23
6	Index	24
7	About the Author	24

Meet Benjamin Franklin.

Benjamin was born on January 17, 1706.

Benjamin grew up in
Boston, Massachusetts.

As a boy, Benjamin worked for his older brother, James.

James owned a printing shop.

Benjamin became a very good **printer**.

Soon, he opened his own printing shop.

He printed books and newspapers.

Poor Richard, 1740.

Polly AN Gillard's

Almanack

For the Year of Chrift

1740,

Being LEAP YEAR.

And makes ſince the Creation	Years.
By the Account of the Eaſtern *Greeks*	7248
By the Latin Church, when ☉ ent. ♈	6939
By the Computation of *W. W.*	5749
By the *Roman* Chronology	5689
By the *Jewiſh* Rabbies	5501

Wherein is contained,

The Lunations, Eclipſes, Judgment of the Weather, Spring Tides, Planets Motions & mutual Aſpects, Sun and Moon's Riſing and Setting, Length of Days, Time of High Water, Fairs, Courts, and obſervable Days.

Fitted to the Latitude of Forty Degrees, and a Meridian of Five Hours Weſt from *London*, but may without ſenſible Error, ſerve all the adjacent Places, even from *Newfoundland* to *South-Carolina*.

By *RICHARD SAUNDERS*, Philom.

PHILADELPHIA:
Printed and ſold by *B. FRANKLIN*, at the New Printing-Office near the Market.

Benjamin loved to read.

He helped start the first **library** in the United States.

DR FRANKLIN
1785

Benjamin was also good at **science**.

He liked to study **electricity**.

Benjamin was also
an **inventor**.

He made special glasses.

They help people see
close-up and far away.

I therefore had formerly two pair of
spectacles which I shifted occasionally
as in travelling sometimes read and
then wanted to regard the Prospects
Finding this change troublesome and not
always sufficiently ready, I had the
Glasses cut, and half of each kind
associated in the same frame, thus

Benjamin was a very good writer, too.

He helped write the **Declaration of Independence**.

Benjamin Franklin did many important things.

We will always remember him.

New Words

Declaration of Independence (dek-luh-**ray**-shuhn **uhv** in-di-**pen**-duhnss) the public statement made on July 4, 1776, in which the American colonies declared themselves free from Great Britain

electricity (i-lek-**triss**-uh-tee) energy that produces heat, light, or motion

inventor (in-**ven**-tuhr) a person who makes or thinks of new things

library (**lye**-brer-ee) a place where books are kept for people to use and borrow

printer (**prin**-tuhr) a person who makes books, magazines, or newspapers

science (**sye**-uhnss) a system of gathering knowledge, using observations and experiments

To Find Out More

Books

A Picture Book of Benjamin Franklin
by David A. Adler
Holiday House

Benjamin Franklin: A Photo-Illustrated Biography
by T. M. Usel
Bridgestone Books

Web Site

The Electric Ben Franklin
http://ushistory.org/franklin/
This site includes a biography of Benjamin Franklin, quotations, a timeline, and fun puzzles and games.

Index

Declaration of Independence, 18

electricity, 14

inventor, 16

library, 12

printer, 10

science, 14

writer, 18

About the Author

Philip Abraham is a freelance writer. He works in New York City.

Reading Consultants

Kris Flynn, Coordinator, Small School District Literacy, The San Diego County Office of Education

Shelly Forys, Certified Reading Recovery Specialist, W.J. Zahnow Elementary School, Waterloo, IL

Sue McAdams, Former President of the North Texas Reading Council of the IRA, and Early Literary Consultant, Dallas, TX